I Am Not Ashamed

A Story of Transformation From A Pedophile's Daughter To A Child of God

by
Susan Maree Jeavons

INTRODUCTION

Lately, I have pondered on what child abuse really does. Not only does it scar the victim, but it scars society. We can see its endless trail of destruction everywhere we look.

A child who has been abused may grow up having a different impression of life than someone who grew up in a loving home. They may be hypersensitive and/or view others with suspicion and caution. They may feel anger, resentment, and even rage towards a society that has failed to protect them. They may withdraw from society because of fear and depression. Or they may fight back by harming themselves and others.

Our jails and prisons are filled with the human wreckage of child abuse and neglect. Many of these criminals were abused as children. Many grew up to become abusers in one way or another, raping, robbing, and wreaking havoc in our communities. Some turn to prostitution or drugs. Still, the full scope of the complications of child abuse is somewhat immeasurable. Its poison has seeped into every corner of society. Yet instead of trying to find solutions to this canker that destroys the spirit of our youth, society has become hyper-violent. In fact, we glamorize violence!

Today's young people view more violence on TV, the Internet, their games, and even in their schools than any generation before them. Violent youth gangs have infected almost every town in America. Young people are told that gangs are cool and are encouraged to join. Many join because they want to feel like they belong, or because they need to be valued for something, even if that something is violence.

Children who have been, or are being abused, may see all this as proof that no one really cares enough to do something to end the violence. But change is needed now! We must care enough to voice our opposition to violence in the media and our communities. We must care enough to teach our children that violence is wrong. We must care enough to turn off the TV, take away the violent games, and take back our cities and towns. We must care enough to stop spoiling our children and start teaching them that they have to work for what they want. We must care enough to stop using our hands to harm, and instead, start extending our hands to help those who need help.

Teaching children the difference between right and wrong may be a basic lesson, yet we have failed to do so adequately. Parenting classes should be mandatory for all high school students. So should relaxation therapy, religion, racial tolerance classes, and self-control classes. Giving our children the education to succeed not only financially in life but personally and spiritually, will hopefully lead to a society that values its children and life itself, more.

Love means caring enough to not only speak out, but to reach out and hold on, and never give up hope on the belief, that all children deserve to live in a violence-free world. Care enough, and it may even lead to world peace someday. That's why I chose to write this book; for the children of the future… RAISE YOUR VOICE. SAVE A CHILD

FORWARD

RAISE YOUR VOICE. SAVE A CHILD. I was too afraid and was threatened, so I kept quiet. What happened? He went on to molest, rape and destroy too many young girls' lives. After my parents died, people started talking, telling me what he did. Turns out he was a pedophile and my own mother knew and stayed married to him for almost 70 years. That's why we moved around so many times! RAISE YOUR VOICE. SAVE A CHILD!

So now I say, RAISE YOUR VOICE. SAVE A CHILD! I am an incest survivor. Some may ask if I had any trepidation about sharing this intimate part of myself. The old wounded me would have cringed away from the truth. The new me, the one with the warrior spirit, demands honesty. No more secrets!

My story is hard to tell, though probably much the same as a lot of survivors. My father sexually abused me from as far back as I can remember, (from about 5 to 17.)

At an early age, I became hyper-vigilant, listening for footsteps, noticing his moods, and watching for any signs of impending danger. The word terror does not do justice to the feelings I had. I remember lying there frightened, waiting, wondering if he'd approach my room or not. If he did, I laid there crying, shivering, eyes closed, trying not to feel, to see. I was too young to understand that what my father was doing was wrong, but I was old enough to feel ashamed.

Now, I am not ashamed. I am an incest survivor. It took me over thirty years to find the courage to say it out loud. Thirty years of struggling with my inner rage and turmoil.

Thirty years to acknowledge that I was not to blame, I had nothing to be ashamed of. Now I am not just a survivor, I am a warrior! I fight against child sexual abuse and exploitation. RAISE YOUR VOICE. SAVE A CHILD

CONTENTS

THE UGLY TRUTH

My father and my mother are gone now. He died of Alzheimer's. She died of COPD and congestive heart failure.

Recently, I discovered that my father had molested many of my cousins and had even raped an aunt who was only 12, but they all will remain unnamed. He also molested a granddaughter, a neighbor girl, and God only knows how many others.

Looking back, I did not know the meaning of pedophile. I thought I was the only one, or that all little girls were treated the same. Many years later, when I learned that my father had molested so many others, I felt guilty for not doing more to make him stop since my mother did nothing. When my mother found out what my father was doing to me, first she called me a liar. Then she wanted me to confront him with her when I got home from roller skating. It was a Friday night and she had found a letter I had written to my boyfriend telling him what my father had done. Friday night I always went roller-skating with Tommy. She wanted me to stay home and for the first time, I screamed and told her no! But when I got home, they were waiting on the couch for me.

Dad wanted to "apologize" to me and promised to leave me alone. That was it! Mom went right back to working nights and leaving me there all night with him. The abuse did not stop until at 17, I got pregnant on purpose to escape from my father. My husband and I stayed together for 9 years and I had three kids. One boy and two girls.

When I look back now, I realize the truth. My mother knew what he was, and that is why she did not sleep with him and why we moved so many times. I do not understand how she could do that to me and still say that she loved him. They were married for 65 years. During those 65 years, they argued constantly. Mom was the instigator; always disagreeing with anything he said.

Dad went to work every day. Although we never had the best shoes or the best clothes, we never went without them. Dad had two personalities. He also had Bipolar. It runs on his side of the family. You could tell what kind of day it was going to be by his moods. I and 2 of my children have it.

HEALING POETRY

The poems in this book were written over a forty-five-year period of transition from victim to survivor. It was not an easy metamorphosis, but then so too, must the butterfly struggle to emerge from his dark cocoon.

Those years of being in my own dark chrysalis were not wasted years. Although they were difficult, they were years of learning, accepting, and evolving into the authentic person I was meant to be.

I did not emerge from that cocoon without any help from the outside world. There were friends and family along the way who encouraged me, comforted me, and allowed me to walk my own path. They were essential to my journey. Without support, the cocoon may be crushed and damaged beyond repair, and the butterfly would never be born.

When we do not face our past, or we pretend that it did not happen, we stifle our spiritual growth. We stop the natural flow of life, and we do the same thing our abusers did, we change who we are. It's as if the butterfly was never meant to exist.

It is my hope that by reading these poems cautiously, by acknowledging your own pain, and by dealing with your own anger and bitterness, you can find the courage to excavate your warrior spirit to speak out, not be ashamed anymore, and emerge from that cocoon to be the beautiful butterfly you were meant to be.

CAUTION-Please make sure that you are emotionally safe and ready before you begin this journey. If you're not sure, find professional guidance first. Some of the poems may be triggering.

The poems featured represent a lifetime of struggle, healing, growth, and reflection. May your transformation finally, give you wings to fly,

Susan Maree
The blank pages are for your journey.

This is me when I was 5. It is hard to look at that picture without grieving, without wondering why my father did what he did, and why my mother did not protect me. Sometimes I look in the mirror and still see that little girl, feel her sadness, her terror, and I ache for her. Now, many years later, that little girl is still with me, the only difference, she is no longer afraid to tell. She is safe at last and she is no longer ashamed.

RAISE YOUR VOICE. SAVE A CHILD!

TRIGGER WARNING

INNOCENCE

In the beginning
there was trust
until
my world changed forever...

TRESPASSER

I watch
the sliver of light
beneath my door

wait
for familiar shadows
to cross my threshold.

Beneath insecure blankets
a silent scream
invasion complete...

INCOMPLETE METAMORPHOSIS

There are days,
when I want to forget,
wipe the slate clean,
become someone new.

There are days when
apple pies and lilac skies
can slightly modify,
yet inside

I am seven
afraid
alone
betrayed...

NIGHT TERROR

The little girl's afraid of the night,
and shadows that move in,
fearful of the awful touch,
the smell of the sickening grin.

She's hiding, hiding, all alone,
waiting for the sun,
never knowing what is real,
wishing she could run...

I remember his whiskey breath. It gagged me. I'd turn my face away and stare out the window.

DELUGE

It Begins
as a rustle of leaves
delicate chimes
then escalates
to waves crashing
and sails thrashing
till calming flood
eases the tide
of sorrow controlled
way too long...

Too many nights I have cried myself to sleep. Even now at 71, I still cry myself to sleep, but for different reasons sometimes. Too many missing children are being trafficked sexually. I can imagine what they are going through, and I pray for them every night.

REFLECTIONS OF ABUSE

We are the quiet ones,
shying away from society,
too afraid to trust,
too afraid to see.

We are the destructive ones,
obliterating whatever gets too close,
numbing our pain with
drugs, obsessions, lies.

We are the creative ones,
twisting words or clay,
painting pictures
that personify our pain.

We are too, survivors,
people who struggle one day at a time,
knowing that nothing could
be as bad as what we've

already survived…

As a writer and poet, I have discovered so many survivors who are incredibly talented, in either writing, painting, or photography.

CHILDHOOD SCARS

They say,
"Time heals all wounds,"
but "they"
were probably never abused.
Those wounds are sometimes
more lethal than a gunshot,
for just when you think
they are healed,
they begin to ooze…

DISTORTED IMAGES

He was nothing-
a shadow,
stranger of pain.

He was shivers
beneath covers,
evil, insane!

He was two people
but very different,
very different those two
black and white
in day or night
and the people never knew
the people never knew...

This poem describes his mental illness bipolar. No one he worked with, none of their friends, even his mother never knew what kind of man he truly was. But I knew, and I know my mother knew.

HELTER-SKELTER

In my mind
there is no silence,
no retreat
from this fated
inner mêlée.

No escape from this
intricate
web of emotion,
only a half-hearted urge
to quiet the past
forever...

May is Mental Health Awareness Month. In my twenties, my Bipolar was just beginning to emerge. I could not shut my brain off. At times I even wanted to end it by suicide. Twice I ended up in the hospital, once for ten days.

TRIGGER WARNING

THE OFFERING

Here Daddy-
take her.
Isn't she pretty?
She looks
a lot like me.
You can
hold her
and squeeze her
and touch her
and she won't cry
or bleed
or tell,

I promise...

EYES SHUT TIGHT

I surrender being,
dissolve
into black hole
of Hudson Street
wonder
if everyone
has this power
to alter the Universe.

Primal fear
forces me to flee
repulsive reality
until Daddy is finished

I breathe
and scrub the truth away...

When my father was doing what he did to me, I would shut my eyes and disappear. Sometimes I'd pretend I was at my Granny's. Other times, at the river. When he was finished, I would take a hot shower. But I never felt clean...

DEATH OF INNOCENCE

I remember, I remember
the fury inside,
the shame that I suffered
when my pain was denied.
I felt like the corpse
of an innocent child.
The instant he touched me
my spirit was defiled.
I remember, I remember,
my cries went unheard
and I will never forget
when the killing occurred…

IN WAITING

In the silence of waiting
my soul craves validation
for all the suffering,
all the pain…

The waiting was waiting for it to end, waiting for my mother to leave him, waiting to just be loved.

POETIC REMEDY

Simple words cannot express
the anguish I have known.
for it goes beyond explanation.
When a child is violated
there is no justification
that alleviates the pain,
no expression that soothes
the fear of betrayal.
Poetry is the only way
of understanding me,
the only way to heal
everything broken
and put this jigsaw puzzle
back in order,
even if some pieces
are still missing…

MUSICAL LOBOTOMY

If I could purge
that part of my brain
which stores pain,

I would replace it
with a gentle refrain
Bach, Beethoven
or simply rain…

PERPETUAL CLEANSING

It is time once more
to scrub every exposed pore,
every wretched, weeping wound.

Steam rises like a magical potion,
surrounds me like a sanitizing rain
that purifies all that is stained.

Salty tears trickle upon tiled floor,
fuse with fetid pieces of the past
until my soul is clean once more.

Still, tomorrow
I will begin the ritual
all over again…

OUT OF REACH

I wish I could remember soft,
gentle touches by loving hands,
affectionate words
spoken without innuendo.

I wish I could recall
a time when innocence
was unbroken
and little hearts still trusted
beyond a shadow of a doubt…

TRIGGER WARNING

THE DAY I WENT FROM HAPPY CHILD TO A FRIGHTENED ANIMAL

Lord knows how many times
I've tried to forget
that exact moment.
I'd rather
walk on hot coals,
eat lye soap,
anything but remember.
Was it the day
a rainbow appeared
in shades of grey,
thunder drowned
out cries
and I faded
into dark corners
where fiends
dared to hide,
Father transformed?

I'd rather walk barefoot
in lightning, sit under a tree
wait for the explosion
to leave ashes
where I used to be,
than remember.

Lord knows I've tried
to forget, tried to erase
the dirty grey matter
from my brain.
I'd rather cover it with

soft, comfortable words
dress it up, pretend
it was someone else
for just a moment
and maybe
I could forget
what terror felt like
that exact moment...

REMNANTS

Up the stairs,
around the corner
and inside a tiny closet
I hid from hostile faces.

Beneath heavy quilts
and heavier burdens
I stashed my secrets
away in guarded places.

In my mind
there was no pain,
and there, no one
could ever hurt me again.

At sixteen
the closet was too small
for so much baggage,
so, I abandoned it all.

At least I thought I did,
until one day,
twenty years later,
I found remnants of it
tucked behind a memory…

BI-POLAR, INSIDE OUT

In this realm of uncertainty
nothing
is taken
at face value.
I examine
and explore,
sift through
and probe
every distorted angle
until the fragments
are turned
inside out
and the jigsaw puzzle
is finally put together
and
truth can no longer hide
in the deep
dark
recesses
of my mind….

FINAL ESCAPE

She is trapped
in the snare of abuse,
not even recognizing
that she is prey.

She is intelligent
but has an excuse
for why he always
treats her this way.

She is in love with a man
who can seduce
and manipulate her
day after day.

She sees no way out,
says "What's the use?"
He'll never change,
though she thinks he may.

And then one night
after more abuse,
she cuts a vein
and slips away.

At last, she is free
from her self-induced
misery…

Suicide is a permanent solution to a temporary problem.
Get help if you are thinking of suicide.
National Suicide Prevention Lifeline
Hours: Available 24 hours. 800-273-8255

THE NEXT MIRACLE

If a surgeon's knife
can remove cancerous cells,
why can't that same knife
eradicate memories of incest
from my brain?
Is my affliction not as deadly?
Is my quality of life
not as important?
Simply identify the flashbacks,
the bitterness and shame.
Cut them out one by one,
separating conscious
from unconscious memories,
evil from good,
until all that is left
is pure me...

UNHINGED

Today, without reason
I am on the brink
of a perilous ravine
hovering between
expectation and desperation,
my head pounding
to the rhythm
of this chaos
called life
every fiber of my being
so tired of the struggle..

PERPETUAL EMOTION

Just when she trusts
the dust has settled on old injuries
a tempest swells
threatens her serenity.

Something triggers
an ancient rage,
a sound, a fragrance,
words on a page.

Sanity walks
a perilous rope.
Psyche struggles
for strands of hope.

She plots
her final wretched breath
welcomes
sweet, merciful death...

TREPIDATION

Memories
insipid and ephemeral,
yet they are capable
of inducing an unshakable dread
of things that should be
long gone...

Suicide is a permanent solution to a temporary problem.
Get help if you are thinking of suicide.
National Suicide Prevention Lifeline
Hours: Available 24 hours. 800-273-8255

IMMORTAL WOUNDS-DAMN THE NIGHT-10/23/98

The dream begins and ends the same each night,
brings back memories she would soon forget.
Terror once suppressed is brought to light.
She fears the nights, forgotten silhouettes.

When morning comes, she poses with a grin,
checks her mask to make sure no one sees
scars that she has hidden deep within,
For Daddy’s little girl must always please!

Damn the shameful night and damn the day!
Hear my cries, allow me to break free!
I will take control! I shall! I may!
If God above can hear my angry plea!

The dream begins and ends the same each night,
terror once suppressed is brought to light...

SHATTERED

She's a dwelling
without foundation.
She's delicate lace
marked "Handle with Care."
She's a fragile vase
with hairline cracks
awaiting restoration...

FLASHBACKS-MODERN STYLE

Like scenes in an old
black and white movie
they turn off
with only one channel
for I've lost
the control switch...

THIS SIDE OF LUNACY

Down is black
silent
lonely,
an empty, aching state.
Up is red
rushing
rambunctious;
no time to hesitate!
Inside, a kaleidoscope
of emotions out of control,
tangled,
twisted,
torturing
the fabric of my soul...

LONGING

I grieve for old things
almost forgotten,
bits and pieces
of gentler days,
days unhurried
by obligations
and design.

I hunt for lost memories
as details fade
into a foggy fantasy
filled with simple truths.
Because somewhere back there
innocence lies in wait
of unthinkable dangers…

FLASHBACK

With a flicker of darkness,
my stomach in knots
and a sense
of overwhelming doom
it starts.
Body shudders, headaches,
fists clench
and my wall breaks
from the weight
of too many memories,
of a child's pain
visions of betrayal
over and over again….

SUICIDE

In the black of night
she slashes a wrist
to bleed herself
of his malignant poison,
then closes her eyes,
and surrenders to the
reruns one more time...

Suicide is a permanent solution to a temporary problem.
Get help if you are thinking of suicide.
National Suicide Prevention Lifeline
Hours: Available 24 hours. 800-273-8255

PROZAC DAZE

The eighties were a haze of
Prozac daze and sleepless nights,
panic-stricken midnight flights!
Razor cuts into the vein,
not to lose, not to gain.
Simply just to ease my pain.
Mania's maddening! Depression kills!
Anti-depressants-Pills! Pills! Pills!
Stomach pumped! Failed again!
Please forgive me for my sin
The psychiatrist says, "Just forget!"
Damn, his wry, sardonic wit!
Once is all I can survive!
When I'm dead, I'm still alive!
End this agonizing phase!
Deliver me from the Prozac daze!

SENSITIVE SIDE

INNER CHILD

Sometimes I cry
for the little girl
who never could.
I see her
there in darkness
waiting for
redemption
waiting for
deliverance
waiting for me
and sometimes
I cry...

JUST BREATHE

Breathing
not an option
as I
lie stiff-legged
feign death,
hope,
he'll go away,
deem me useless
as he often states
through clenched teeth.
Inhale
nauseating scent,
till my stupor
hastens his exit
and I exhale...

SHATTERED SIDE

Fragile-handle
with care, for she's
soft as new grass
on bare feet

before weeds
force their way up
prick tender toes
and she recoils

until scars tougher
than nails form
callous calluses
on her soul...

FRAGMENTS

I saw her once
from a distance
sad, blue eyes crying.
She never knew
how much I ached
to hold her
comfort her
protect her from the night.

From a distance
I saw her once
there inside of me...

INQUISITIVE SIDE

I search for answers
in mysterious spaces
places where shadows
lurk waiting for me.

I search for answers
without and within
on this life-long journey
fate compels me to win.

Mysteries are hidden
deep in my breast,
I question my conscience
expose the suppressed

but the answers are lost
somewhere in my mind
secrets we share-
never defined.

BORDERLINE

A one minute
commercial about Daddies,
little girls and puppies
arouses jealousy, tears,
then a familiar bile
that rises up, threatens
to spew vile emotions
laying just beneath
surface of sanity.

INTRICATE DESIGNS

Being a child
in stretched-out skin
I fear unworthiness
shy away from conflict
retreat into
the safe world of poetry
where I can be real,
no need for obscurity
until the burden of truth
creeps in, frightens,
and I crawl further
into me...

AT THE EDGE...1998

Sometimes, it feels like I'm
right back where I started from,
alone and needing to be loved so much.
Maybe that's why I'm still searching,
searching in forests, searching in fields,
searching in faces, yet never quite knowing
what it is I'm trying to find.
Sometimes, life feels so hopeless,
so pointless, so ethereal,
as I stand at the edge and wait...

TIGHT SPOT

Claustrophobia,
caused by a
suffocating fog,
induces visions
of a closet were
she used to hide from
shadows in the night...

STILL WAITING

Telling me
to let go of the past
is like asking me
to stop breathing.
The past leaches out
of every pore,
peeks out
from every corner
waiting
to strike again
when I least expect,
waiting to destroy
my whisper of serenity...

PRIMAL RAGE

This feral urge to scream
surfaces from somewhere
beneath layers
of resistance,
and threatens
to spew secrets
once sedated by time...

MIGRAINE

I sense a subtle change,
climatic pressure
settles in my brain

Demons dance,
stomp in defiance.

Depression descends
like a downhill train,
hurls me into a haze of pain
as I pull the shades,
surrender to the pressure...

EXPOSE

They thought I'd keep quiet
but I fooled them.
Secrets exposed
in black and white
for all the world to see.
Still, I remain
anonymous...

Grand Finale

Her secrets shrouded
in streaks of ink
traces of shame
on pale parchment sail
eloquent farewell...

BETRAYAL

In the darkness of secrecy
a child is betrayed
and a once cheerful haven
becomes her prison...

RUNAWAY

Going nowhere so fast
my head spins
in a manic flurry
that ends
when I crash
into me...

REDEMPTION

This paper and this pen
are Band-Aids that
must be changed daily
to keep the flesh from
contaminating the psyche,
infecting the spirit.
I write because I can,
because I must!
For if I do not,
then I have no design,
only blank pages filled with misery,
filled with black memories
and festering scars
that never heal...

ABSENT

There is no proof
only
ever-present truth
memories
close-at-hand,
fear I don't understand
and when I close my eyes
darkness verifies
I wasn't really there
cause no one heard my cries...

SHADOWS OF TERROR

Familiar shadows pass my room,
warn me of impending doom.
In the darkness lie awake,
pray the Lord my soul will take.

Shake and shiver, hide my head,
sometimes wish that I were dead!
Cry out in my sleep at night;
Please, Dear God! This isn't right!

Wait for morning light to shine;
everything will be just fine.
Fear the shadow's here to stay;
steals my innocence away!

DESPERATION

I'm rocking, rocking
day and night,
staring blankly
black and white
no emotions
no more fight.
Emptiness
drains my soul
no more passion
no more goals.
Death is waiting
within me
Do not enter
hear my plea
I'm alone
with reality

THE COLLECTOR

I have a need
to gather together
a tidy, tangible
representation
of all that was wholesome
and normal in my childhood.

A twenty-year search
nets teddy bears,
dolls, books, and toys
that gave comfort
to an abused child
when nothing else would.

Now,
surrounded
by treasures of my past,
I still
yearn
for more...

FAIR GAME

When I was younger
I bared my soul,
wore my heart
with directions on my sleeve.

Like a sitting duck
going nowhere,
I was easy prey-
Ping! Ping! Bullseye!
Give that man his prize!

SUPPORT GROUP

Smiling,
telling stories,
concealing
wounds

an arduous meeting
of strangers united
by malignant
circumstances.

They size each other up,
test the water
with bent elbows
inherent suspicion intact

wait for each
to bare their scars
wonder whose knife
cut deeper...

JUST ONCE

Just once, I want to wake
and not remember,
see in the mirror
clues of my past.

Just once I want to dream,
not scream in terror.
I want to cry, know someone
cares at last.

Just once I want to hope
tomorrow's different,
just once, Oh Lord,
just once...

SHELTERED SIDE

Emotions simmer behind
thick layers set in stone
impenetrable walls
created long ago.

Thick layers set in stone
to keep the pain away
created long ago
walls that won't decay.

To keep the pain away
to hide reality
walls that won't decay
stay in this shell called me.

To hide reality
assure my sanity
stay in this shell called me
stay in this shell called me.

THE MISCHIEVOUS SIDE

Conniving, hating,
contemplating
evil thoughts and deeds
She's there, I know
she's waiting there
to plant her loathsome seeds.

Immoral notions,
pernicious potions
all a part of me
She's there, I know
she's waiting there
Deep inside of me...

IN BLOOD ONLY…
POEMS ABOUT FAMILIES
&
BETRAYAL

The following poems relate how it feels to be abused, neglected, and betrayed by those who were supposed to love and protect you.

EXTRACTION

She makes excuses
for my brother's cruelty,
blames it on unsubstantiated
brain damage at birth.
She talks about her
near-death experience
during my cesarean delivery
never once offering justification
for our lack of bonding...

MOTHER

I have no memories of you,
only glimpses.
We are familiar
yet still there remains
an emptiness,
a hollow place
where I know you should be
holding, protecting me

from shadows of the night.

EXTREME JUSTICE

Purge this poison
from my soul
still my body
calm my cries

Psychopath
in control
cleanse toxins
of father's lies

Scalpel cuts
venom streams
no excuse
no alibis

Close my eyes
hear his screams

Oh, sweet justice
satisfies!

This was written about a dream I had of murdering my father. Of course, I didn't.

DETACHED

She must have been absent
when I was born

or maybe it was simply
a bad connection

a loose umbilical cord

for I was a child
on my own

from day one...

IRREVERENCE, UNREFINED

He says grace the same
every time,
and with each breath
I chew louder,
mock his phony litany
ward off
yet another violation.

He slings scripture
in my face
pretends
nothing happened
threatens
hell, fire, and damnation
if I don't obey my "father".

In unison, he, and Mama
say "Amen"
flash disapproval
as I belch obnoxiously
leave the dinner table
gratified, before
they've begun...

I did not act like this. I was too afraid to. But I thought about it...

BABYSITTER

She wore spicy red lipstick,
dirty blond hair
smelled of B.O. and garlic
but made the best
chocolate chip cookies.

Her stomach billowed
over callused knees.
She chain-smoked,
struggled to breathe
but her voice; gentle as an angel's.

She brought
fairy tales to life,
offered healing praise
until in walked Mama
breaking the magic spell...

CONTRABAND

He's seventy-two,
brings me peace offerings
pathetic trinkets meant
as atonement for transgressions
he could never explain.

I brusquely feign gratitude
wait for him to leave,
shamelessly deposit
his trivial tokens in the trash
exoneration renounced...

SHAME

Can I paint darkness
the right shade of terror,
that precise scent of you?

Will I know the truth
if my heart beats
to the rhythm of deceit?

How will I behave
if my body craves fire
beneath a traitor moon?

Where will I see light
if your shadow is cast
in every corner of the night?

Tell me, Daddy,
what kind of woman will I be
with your stench on me?

BLANKS

Simply
blanks

no negatives
or flashbacks
to jar my memory

nothing but space
where you
should have been

loving
nurturing
caring at all
Mama...

CRUCIAL DISTRACTION

If I stare at the ceiling
long enough,
I become the ceiling

rise above this pain,
above
this black abyss

of terror...

COUNTERFEIT BONDS

Innocence is my defense,
a little child can
make no sense,
cannot relate to
hate and vile.
Mama, may we reconcile?

Only lies and alibis,
you never touched
or heard my cries
never stopped
to see the truth
naiveté of your own youth.

Still, I search
for consolation.
Was I but a
complication?
Were you ever
fond of me?
Mama, you never once told me...

FULL LOAD

If I could bleach away
the stains of you,
scrub and scrub until
not one hint of you remains,
then I could dry out my brains
and feel clean again…

I NEVER KNEW

I never knew
those other little girls
didn't play
the same games
that you and I played
Daddy.

I never knew
that hugs and kisses
could be good things
and that there was
any such thing
as "bad" touches.

I never knew
how much I hated you
until Haleigh
smiled at me
and said,
"I love you, Grandma."

EXORCISING MAMA

I cannot remember you, Mama.
When I close my eyes
you are never there;
always missing in action.

I have wasted hours,
days, eternity
searching for you, trying
to recreate your image.

I cannot feel
your arms around me,
hear your voice easing my fears,
singing me a lullaby.

Maybe I tucked you away,
kept you in some dark corner
where I hid my shame,
my secrets.

Still,
you manage to slip out
Mama,
when I least expect

a face in the mirror
frightfully familiar...

MAMA

I wanted your approval,
did little things to make you proud
but you never once praised me,
never once celebrated my existence.
I longed to be the favored child,
to be embraced by you.
I patiently waited, Mama
but you never came
and your indifference
still makes me shiver...

SHADES OF MAMA

She wrapped garbage
in old newspaper,
wore pin curls
to drive-in movies.

She ate everything in sight,
smoked Lucky Strikes,
complained
about chest pain.

On Tuesday nights
she bowled in a league,
leaving me alone,
defenseless.
Then again
Mama
never cared
for trivial matters...

THE NIGHTMARE

Lights go out, she starts to shake, she knows what happens then.
He'll come into her room and the nightmare will begin!
She'll close her eyes real tight, pretend that she's asleep,
maybe he will leave if she doesn't make a peep,
but he knows she's awake and says, "Daddy won't hurt you,
cause you're Daddy's little girl and I know you love me too.
Don't let Mommy hear us. She'll get mad at me,
so be Daddy's little girl, and be quiet as can be."

The little girl's confused doesn't know what's real,
doesn't understand the way her Daddy makes her feel.
She loves him and she hates him, and longs to tell someone,
but Mommy never listens and there's nowhere she can run!
Now the little girl's a woman, with a family of her own
and there's a man who says he loves her every night when they're alone.

The lights go out, she starts to shake, she knows what happens then,
he'll come into her room and the nightmare will begin,
the nightmare will begin…

This is the very first poem I wrote about my abuse. I think I was about 17.

BARE NECESSITIES

When other mothers stayed home,
I knew why you worked the graveyard shift;
separate bedrooms locked tight
angry words; evidence of infidelity.
Your absence left me vulnerable
with no one to tuck me in,
listen to my prayers.

Oh, how I prayed Mama,
all the while hyper-vigilant
to Daddy's footsteps,
sickening scent of whiskey,
as he, in the name of love,
took my innocence
under cover of darkness.

Each year, in exchange for your betrayal,
I received three plaid, cotton dresses for $7.98.
I chewed their collars, hid behind them,
fearful other children saw through
to where shame dripped like acid rain
exposing my dirty secrets.

Now, my daughter wears velvet and lace.
At night, I rock her to sleep.
At night, I am there.

Today, she thanked me.
We held each other and I cried
for all we could have had
Mama...

Bare Necessities after the last quatrain, Your Family and Betrayal

Use this page to tell how your family betrayed you.

POEMS ABOUT OUR WARRIOR SPIRIT

I am a new person. I am stronger, wiser, more courageous, and more compassionate.

The following poems show how victims can begin to heal, gain strength, and fight back by becoming warriors who speak out and help other survivors.

SACRED CIRCLE

We gather here
to share our pain,
our hopes,
our dreams
and our victories.
We are survivors
who have been
to hell
and back again;
robbed of innocence.

Now,
after years of struggle
we at long last
raise our voices
in unison
reveal our secrets
without shame or fear,
to heal our wounds
and our spirits
together
here in this sacred circle...

A MIGHTY FORCE

For so long, we believed that we alone
were the only ones who knew
the disgrace of our reality
and what we had been through.

We hung our heads in silent shame
and never told a soul.
We kept our secrets locked inside
and never quite felt whole.

Then one day a stranger came to us
and whispered secrets kept.
Together we learned to trust again,
together we both wept.

At last, we are a mighty force,
survivors who stand tall,
speak out against all child abuse,
demand justice for us all!

THERAPEUTIC INK

My blood
runs across the page
as memories in indigo.

Each drop, each line
validates my existence,
liberates me from the past

strengthens my will to go on.

HEALING STEPS

For a long time
I couldn't find her.
She was lost somewhere
between innocence and shame.

Sometimes, I catch
a glimpse of her,
reach out to her
and call her name

but she ran away
still afraid to trust.
Little by little
we conquered the past.

Now, we walk
hand-in-hand,
heart-to-heart,
together at last...

SECRETS

We were told to never tell.
Now we shout it to the world!

Never again,
will darkness hide our truth!

Never again
will our spirits be imprisoned!

We, now masters of our souls,
soar on wings
rightfully earned.

SURVIVAL OF THE FITTEST

Even a tree
must struggle to survive,
tossed and torn
in the wind and rain,
yet it grows stronger
and begins to thrive,
becoming greener
for all its pain.

METAMORPHOSIS

After the anger
threatened to devour me,
I escaped
the abyss of desolation
by reaching inside to were
the broken spirit of a child cried.

Comforting her
I realized
how long we had suffered,
all we had lost,
how tough we must
have been to survive.

Once
I nurtured her,
assured her of my devotion
we rose beyond the sorrow,
discovered serenity

on brand new wings…

THE CIRCLE OF DEVOTION

I am fortunate to call you, my friend.

When we found each other
it was as if we were brought together
to comfort, give hope
to those who felt alone,
offer our hands and hearts
in friendship, to those
still learning to trust.

Together we have created
a sacred circle of healing,
a refuge where we are
free to be authentic,
free to renew our spirit.

Each step we take
is a milestone,
a mountain we climb together,
and together, we will go
with courage...

RESIDUE

I put them in with Thursday's trash,
there in the bottom of the old rusty can
beside rancid fat and burned succotash,
remnants of youth I would rather forget.

Mixed with bits of shattered glass,
lie broken promises and things I regret.
Toss in one final wretched mass-
flashbacks wrapped in guilt and shame.

Close the lid, and lock it tight.
Time to end this dreadful game.
Now dance the healing dance tonight,
Now dance the healing dance tonight…

THINGS LEFT BEHIND

Like unclaimed pawn
I lay no claim
to the toxic debris
you left behind.

Your attempts to maim
are erased now-gone.
My spirit is free,
my truth re-defined…

TURNING POINT

For years, my life
was a dreadful song
and I danced an agonizing
dance of self-destruction.

Now I realize
that I deserve serenity.
Now I choose a different song,
dance to a different beat

and the music,
the sweet, sweet music
replenishes my soul
and I can dance

and I can dance…

SECURING THE LEAD

A lifetime ago
others
directed my fate
composed each episode
methodical contempt
consistently dispensed
in small lethal doses.

Now
I excavate the antidote
enclosed in innocence,
a cure once concealed

behind illusions and deceit,
truth dispensed
in revitalizing doses..

INNER HEALING

What secrets did you keep?
Oh, child of mine?
What terrors in your sleep
did life define?

What hopes and dreams
did destiny deprive?
How you had to scheme
to just survive.

Wherever you are now,
I hope you know
I'll hold your hand,
protect you from the foe.

Oh, little one
you need not be afraid,
together we will
let the old wounds fade.

IN THE NAME OF DIGNITY

We have struggled
to get where we are,
told secrets to spite those
who warned us not to tell.

We fought for balance
in an unstable world,
concealed our misery
in a reality of hell.

Now we stand
unbound,
united in spirit
on sacred ground.

SURVIVOR'S DECREE

Just because your past caused pain
and night reminds you of terror's reign,
it does not mean you can't survive.
It only means that you're alive.

The worst is over, you lived to tell
about the time you spent in hell.
Now stand up tall and stand up proud!
We are survivors! No victims allowed!

AFFIRMATION

Call me a survivor. Call me a woman.
Call me a fighter and sacred muse.
I am courageous. I am persistent.
I am strong, win or lose.
I am a warrior. I am a mother.
I am set loose forever more.
I fought the battle, stayed the course
and at last, my struggles were over.

ANONYMOUS CHILD

Too long we were silent, too long we cried.
You refused to listen. Too many died!

For too long you turned and would not see
the truth of our reality.

No more we'll hide the facts from you!
The World will know what we've been through!

We'll stand up proud and publicize
the evil that the world denies!

We now reclaim what was defiled!
We are the voice of an anonymous child!

RESOLUTION

I will not be silenced!
I will not be ashamed!
I will hold my head high,
my hips unrestrained.

I will tell all your secrets,
I will not be afraid.
I am not your prisoner.
I will not be swayed.

I will speak of the truth
in blood, black, and white
I will never be subdued
or surrender this fight.

SECOND CHANCE DANCE

I wear passionate purple
when they expect me to wear
subdued, mediocre white.

I dance barefoot in the rain
bare-breasted and unashamed
alone in the heat of night.

I celebrate and I cry
I'm reborn before I die
and reclaim what once was mine

with innocent delight.

IN THE FEELING

There is a terror
in the remembering,
a terror of the truth,
a terror of the unknown
and the known.

There is a settling
in the knowing,
a settling of my inner spirit
when accepting my setbacks,
my weaknesses, my victories.

There is a cleansing
in the grief,
a cleansing of the toxins
that pervaded my existence,
threatened my sanity.

There is a freedom
in the telling,
freedom from a lifetime
of secrecy and lies,
shame and silence.

There is a healing
at long last,
healing of body, mind, and spirit,
born of determination, courage, and hope
healing, at long last

a hard-fought-for healing...

VULNERABLE

Walk for a while
listen and hear
echoes of anguish
rumblings of fear

Cautiously now
trusting takes space
suspicions remain
innately in place

Here beside me
an equal you'll find
never in front
never behind

Walk on this path
soon you will see
indications of healing
a spirit set free...

CRIMSON

A poor excuse is better than the truth
Red, the color of anger, youth
Red rivers of rage ran through my veins
Red, the color of shameful stains
Now I wear red to defeat the past
bright, bold, scarlet
me at last!

ACT ONE

This lifetime
is simply a rehearsal.

In my next gig
I will sing opera
or dance seductively
with a handsome stranger.

In my next life
I will sip margaritas
on a deserted island
and never feel alone.

I will never know
the feeling of being betrayed.
I will not have to imagine
a world without child abuse

For my next gig
the world will be a perfect place
where suffering and hate
aren't even in the dictionary…

ACCEPTANCE

There is a settling occurring
Deep within my soul,
a tranquil repose
long-awaited.

It is a purging
which empowers my spirit
to proclaim
its desire

and accept destiny
with open arms…

FROM WOMAN TO CRONE

There is peace in my aloneness now,
unlike when I was a young woman
whose seclusion almost drove her mad.
I used to believe that I had wasted
so much time, until at last,
I understood the lessons.

These wrinkles you see,
they are all a part of me
and with the passage of time
and the acceptance of memories,
both bitter and sweet, healing began
and wisdom was born out of misery.

SACRED RITE

In silence
I hear music

melancholy melodies
washing gracefully
through ancient corridors,

waves of rhythm
drifting across
gently rolling green.

When I close my eyes,
cosmic light
leads the way

to Shangri-La,
where someday,
in ceremonial display,

I shall surrender
to the Gods,
dance naked in the rain

celebrate survival
unafraid…

THINGS NEEDING DONE

Just once
I want to forget
that the past is real
and pretend
that I am unscarred,
invincible.

Just once
I need to take a chance,
dance wildly upon
green, green meadows
where fescue and bluebells
blow in a soft Carolina breeze.

Just once
I need to be strong enough
to climb Grandfather Mountain,
stand on his peaks
and shout to the gods,
"I am free!"

EVIDENCE

Without warning
I am consumed
by an uncontrollable urge
to prowl childhood corridors
once uncontaminated.

With pen in hand
I recount details
once forgotten,
accentuate to validate
things left unspoken...

TRANSFORMATION

From the daughter of darkness
to a woman of light,
I searched for my soul
to make everything right.
I suffered in silence,
too long I was still
now I shout out the truth
and it helps me to heal.
My secrets no longer
have any control.
Now I am the master
of my own soul
and finally, finally
this woman is whole.

TRUE REFLECTIONS

In the mirror, I see a face
that's sometimes tired and old.
Her life at times, a brutal race
really took its toll.
The face I see does not reveal
the secrets hidden there,
for they are veiled behind the mask
that she prefers to wear.
The person that she has become
is one who knows much grief,
but she has made the best of life,
and at last, has found relief
in all the little blessings
that God has brought about.
Now when she sees her image
she finally has no doubt
that the woman in the mirror
is a strong but gentle soul,
and the reflection smiling back
is at long last, finally whole.

COSMIC CRONE

Alone
beneath
umbrella of lilacs,
moonbeams

I meditate
contemplate
how infinitesimal
we are.

While
entranced
by nature's symphony
a revelation

women
are the essence of life
guardians of the Universe,
spirit of heaven and earth,

yesterday
today
always...

SECRETS

I was told to never tell.
Now I shout it to the world!
Never again,
will darkness hide my truth!
Never again,
will my spirit be imprisoned!
I am a woman,
master of my soul,
soaring on wings
rightfully earned

I, A Woman

I, a woman
crave a warm embrace,
a smile, a gentle touch,
a tranquil inner space.

I, a woman
survived the dreadful past,
mourned my treasures lost,
but healed my wounds at last.

I, a woman
forever hold the key
that unlocks the fear inside,
controls my destiny.

I, a woman
can change the circumstances,
subdue the evil power,
save by choice not chance.

I, a woman
braved reality,
hence embrace the praise,
now cry, oh victory!

UNFETTERED

I'm unfettered
---------------------O unleashed
unimpeded
by . . . . .time!
I've weathered the storm !!!**#*,

with b.
m
to i
s l
n c
i
a
t
n
u
o
m

Yes at last I am free
no price on my soul,
unfettered, unleashed,
unbroken, and whole!

I AM THE TREE

The tree is bare,
her leaves are gone,
now all that's left,
is what she has on.

Her courage alone
will see her through,
no camouflage
to hide the view.

For all her struggle
she will see
someday she'll be
a stronger tree…

EARTH MOTHER

I am the tree
standing tall and proud.

I am the river,
reflecting every cloud.

I am the mountain
rising to the sky.

I am a woman
and with earth, identify.

REFLECTIONS

It is hard to look at that picture
without grieving, without wondering
why my father, did what he did,
why my mother did not protect me.
Sometimes, I look in the mirror
and still see that little girl,
feel her sadness,
ache for her.
But I'm all grown up
and you can't go home again,
no matter how much
you want a second chance,
a chance to tell them
what could have been;
A chance to be me-
loving, funny, and full of life!
Now, over 60 years later,
that little girl is still with me,
the only difference
she is no longer afraid...

SURFACING

Depression settles in
like it belongs

tries to take over
but I fight back

reject its claim
on my soul.
I will survive...
Your Warrior Spirit
Tell us about your warrior spirit.

AN APPEAL TO SOCIETY

The following poems are written for a society that
sometimes fails
to act to prevent the sexual abuse of children.

PLEASE DON'T HURT ME ANYMORE

Please don't yell. Please don't shout.
I promise I won't cry or pout...
I am just a little child;
now my spirit is defiled.

Please don't hit. Please don't curse.
Don't molest or even worse.
I am little, can't you see
what abuse can do to me?

Please don't kill. Please don't maim,
I'm not always the one to blame.
I am small and can't fight back
when you kick, punch, or smack.

Please be kind. I'll be good
like you and Mommy say I should.
I won't cry. I won't tell,
even when it seems like hell.

Please don't hurt me anymore,
Please don't hurt me anymore...

PLEA FOR MERCY

How can you justify the misery?
Of little ones so innocent and pure?
What logic is behind brutality?
Is evil something we must all endure?

If there's a better place beyond this earth
where misery and suffering disappears,
why must we bear this pain from time of birth
until the ocean fills up with our tears.

Lord, I ask for kindness with these prayers,
from children who call out to you at night.
Dear God, they need to know that someone cares,
these angels who are precious in your sight.

Deliver us from evil, I implore
Oh God in heaven, we can't take much more…

SONNET #3

"How long," I say, "How long will you ignore
the weeping of the children in the night-
the suffering, why do you not abhor,
you the guardians of their inner light?

The angels weep alone, yet no one heeds
not even the almighty God above,
a soul is lost forever, ever bleeds,
cries in silence only seeking love.

With the blood of their innocence upon you,
to mark you as the one who wounds their core,
may God above never offer mercy to you,
but cast you into torment ever more.!"

Humanity will someday pay the cost.
The tragedy is all that we have lost!

DO YOU REMEMBER ME?

You heard me cry, I know you did,
but I am just a little kid.
You turned your back and walked away,
"It's not my problem," I heard you say.

You saw my scars with your own eyes,
but won't admit what it implies.
You're blinded by what others think,
you walked right by and did not blink.

You spoke my name but never knew
the suffering that I've gone through.
You didn't care enough about me
to defend my right to equity.

Why can't you stop and lend a hand,
speak out for me, and take a stand?
I am a child, why can't you see,
that you were once a child like me?

Remember me each night, each day
and if you have the time to pray
ask God to end this violence,
the slaughter of our innocence.

MERCILESS

You tell us to go on,
forget yesterday,
but sometimes
we're still a child
whose scars won't go away.

You tell us we should trust,
and that's so hard to do,
for in the past
your promises
were meaningless to you.

You tell us to forgive,
let the creator be our guide,
but in our prayers
he never heard
the many tears we cried.

You say you understand
but come and walk with me,
then you will know
our burden's power
for all eternity.

You tell us time heals,
for some that may be so,
but in our dreams
the past is now
and we have miles to go,
we have miles to go...

THEY CALL IT "DOMESTIC" VIOLENCE

Today somewhere, someone
will aim a gun to end a life,
or raise a fist to abuse a wife.
They'll not give thought
to consequence.
They think they act
in self-defense.
They seek to destroy
what gets in their way.
They look at life
as a game to play.
There is no conscience
in the soul of the man
who abuses another
with words or hands.

HEALING RAVE

For years, I was always
on the verge of opening up
the floodgates of emotion
that had been held back
for too long by responsibility,
shame and hope

hope that one day
the memories would disappear,
dissipate into thin air
as if they had never been,
as if I were still innocent,
still a child just wanting to be loved.

Thirty years later the floodgates
still hold, and no one knows
the force behind those walls
built from rage and tenacity,
my bleeding spirit scarred
but not broken, determined to survive

in an apathetic world
in which pedophiles
and predators still thrive
behind closed doors
where they breed victims,
disguised as offspring…

BACKLASH

You may see our faces every day
but you never see inside
to the misery and memories
of the fears and tears we hide.

You may recognize our proper names
yet you still may not discern
who we really are, and just how far,
we have journeyed just to learn.

We're your neighbor, friend, associate.
We are refugees from hell
but you just see what you want to see,
and ignore us when we tell.

Don't you hear? Is it the truth you fear?
All your alibis are lame.
We have known abuse. There's no excuse
to believe we were to blame.

Does it nauseate you to know our fate?
Does society atone
for the pain, lies, and the stolen lives,
for the scars of wars, we own?

Don't turn your back! It's not white and black
but true colors that show through
in how you negate, yes even hate
our sincerity with you.

You can't hide the truth of our lost youth.
It will show its face someday,
when the wounds show, everyone will know,
everyone will have to pay…

© 2004 Susan Maree Jeavons - I always think of all the school shootings when I read this. We never know what caused these shooters to break...

SOCIETY'S CHILD

We're the children in the shadows,
battered, broken, and abused!
We're your neighbors,
we're your conscience!
We are raped! We are bruised!
When we cry out, do you hear us?
Does it matter what we feel?
Does your apathy protect you
from our miserable appeals?
Preachers, teachers, politicians,
doctors, lawyers, rich or poor,
all your promises are empty
when our suffering is ignored!
All your laws and propositions
only candy coats the truth
of the countless hideous crimes
perpetrated on our youth!
In a world that's always changing,
child abuse will still remain,
if you cannot feel our hopelessness,
if you do not feel our pain!

DELIVER US FROM EVIL

Dear Lord, we come to you tonight
to ask that you will heed
this prayer we pray 'most every night.
We have a special need.

There are children who are crying, Lord,
afraid to go to sleep,
afraid that you will let us down,
afraid to make a peep.

We hide beneath the covers
awaiting morning light,
praying that you'll save us, Lord
from demons in the night.

We pray for you to love us
and keep us safe from sin.
Some even pray to never wake
from this war we cannot win.

Dear Lord, we pray you'll listen
to each and every prayer.
It's not enough to say you love us,
please prove to us you care

and deliver us from evil Lord,
let innocence prevail.
Dear Lord, we come to you tonight
and plead you do not fail.

Amen

PANTOUM-BLACK AND WHITE REFLECTIONS

Old black and white pictures are faded and worn
the pain they portray is there in her eyes.
Innocence doomed from the time she was born,
no tears for a childhood she lost in the night.

The pain they portray is there in her eyes,
no smiles for this stranger, no secrets revealed.
No tears for a childhood she lost in the night,
the terror is present, but her lips are sealed.

No smiles for this stranger, no secrets revealed,
she looks at the camera and waits for the light.
The terror is present, but her lips are sealed
she must never tell of the hideous night.

She looks at the camera and waits for the light,
not trusting this stranger who stares at her eyes
she must never tell of the hideous night,
the promise of love conceals many lies.

Not trusting this stranger who stares at her eyes
she hurries away when the stranger is done.
The promise of love conceals many lies,
forever she's cursed to invent alibis.

The promise of love conceals many lies,
Old black and white pictures are faded and worn
Innocence doomed from the time she was born,
forever she's cursed to invent alibis...

SCRUPLES

You say you don't want to see
so you shut your eyes to reality.
You never listen when you hear me cry
then you make excuses, weak alibis.

I'm not asking for control,
some give and take is a simple goal.
Morality is a worthy choice
if you listen to your inner voice.

Go on, pretend that I don't exist
but try to keep me quiet and I'll resist!
I'll shout and scream till you finally hear.
I'm your conscience, your heart, your greatest peer.

CONSIDER THE CHILD

When you look into her eyes
try to envision
the fear that she hides,
the pain she endures,
the hope that she holds onto.

When you look into her eyes
consider all that she will become,
consider the memories
that she will live with,
because how you treat her
will affect her forever….

Children, Handle with Care!

THE VOICE OF ANGEL'S

You wonder why I want to die
but never stop to ask me why.
Well listen close and you might hear
the reason for my earthly fear.
You look at me as property,
not just the child that I should be.
I'm new to this and have to learn,
You had your chance, now it's my turn
to run and play and discover me.
It is my life, my destiny.
I make mistakes just like you did
when you were just a little kid,
but you hit and hurt and call me bad,
and when you do it makes me sad.
I tried so hard to do as you say.
At last, you took my hope away,
so I'll be gone when you awake-
I prayed the Lord my soul would take.
It's not that heaven was ready for me,
but I was tired of trying to be
the perfect child,
I was only three...

THE CHILD I USED TO BE

When I think back to a long time ago
and the child I used to be,
I'm saddened by all that she never had,
all the dreams that she'll never see.

Still, a long time ago has come and gone
and the child I used to be
now sets her hopes on different dreams,
and I admire what she's given me.

She gave me the courage to never quit,
and the strength to fight my foes.
She taught me determination
to survive life's highs and lows.

She taught me to care about others,
not to wallow in misery
about something that happened a long time ago
to the child, I used to be.

For without adversity and injustice
that we suffer when innocent,
we would never appreciate our victories-
the spirit of hope they represent.

So, if you look in the mirror someday
and reflect on a long time ago,
be grateful to the child you used to be
for teaching you all that you know.

PEDOPHILE

Devious vermin leave a cruel trail
As they steal their victim's soul.
Innocent prey, tiny, frail.
Never again quite whole,
never again quite whole…
© 2021 SMJ

I AM THE CHILD

You and I have never met
But I am the child you must not forget.
I am the child who whimpered in pain.
I am the child who was beaten and slain.
I am the child who cried at night.
I am the child whose future was bright.
I am the child whose fear was real.
I am the child whose scars won't heal.
I am the child you see each day,
Who is not your problem, so you turn away.
I am the child, the child so small
Who only wanted to be loved, that's all.
You and I have never met,
But I am the child you must not forget.

Poems About Hope and Faith

I wrote this poem in 2001 when I was invited to The Capital of North Carolina to read a poem at a vigil about child abuse. My late, best friend Jackie took me there and when we walked to see the Capital where I would be reading, there were a dozen or so tiny t-shirts strung across the Capital steps. I went back to my hotel and started to write a new poem. After I finished, I read it and knew the words came from God. When Jackie and I got to the vigil, it was so cold I was shivering. It was my nerves too, so I prayed and asked God to calm me and warm me so I could read the poem. I did a good job and thanked him for answered prayers. Since then, the poem has been used in different Child Abuse Prevention campaigns and even in a workbook for adults who were sexually abused as children in Australia.

Your Appeal to Society

Use this page to appeal to society.

Poems About Hope and Faith

The following poems are about my faith in God,
and the hopes I have for the future.

WAKEUP CALL

I close my blinds
take the phone
off the hook
shut out all life.
Inside
I feel like
curling into me
hiding from reality
until one persistent Robin
promises hope
outside my window.

MIND'S EYE

The memories are fading now,
what's left is black and white,
but I see rainbows in my mind
and angels in the light.
A rose in bloom, a Winter Day,
a little hand in mine;
wisdom tells me all of this
was part of God's design.
A starry night, a sunny day,
now a little child to hold;
I close my eyes and I am young
and never will grow old
never will grow old...

DEPARTURE

It is time we say
goodbye, old friend.

Too long
we have suffered together.

Too long
our characters have clashed

You hiding from the pain,
Me fighting to end it.

Goodbye, dreadful yesterdays.
Hope knows only tomorrow…

MILES TO GO...

Try to understand
this woman I am
for sometimes I'm not sure
I even know.

I've come a long, long way
from the roads of yesterday,
still, there are many miles
I must go,
so many, many
miles I must go...

ON WINGS OF TIME

I turned 55 recently
and still, I find myself
reflecting, wondering
who and where I would be today
if life had been different.

Maybe I'll never know
why it happened to me
or maybe the answers,
consecrating my struggles,
are here in black and white.

Thirty-four years ago
I began my healing journey.
It has taken all that time
to at last find my spirit,
exercise my still, fragile wings.

Today, I look in the mirror,
see no martyr,
but a survivor who cares,
someone who knows where you've been
and how far you can fly
if you only try...

INTERNAL BLEEDING

Deep in her solar plexus
memories stab away
trying to destroy
her fragile thread of sanity

until somewhere inside
a small voice says,
"Enough!
I want to live,"

and hope is born...

DESPERATION

Days of nothingness
settle in like rheumatism
aching deeper with age

no soothing balm for my spirit,
no healing potion to ease my pain,
only the promise of tomorrow.

HOMAGE

To those who went before me
And felt the evil hand,
To those who hid in silence
And never took a stand,

For this, I shall pay homage
And let your names be heard.
Your sacrifice was not in vain,
I give you all my word.

I honor all your heartache
And your painful history.
I've felt your emptiness,
your shame and misery.

Childhood should be sacred.
Little children should not die.
Hands should never hurt you
Or make you run and cry.

So, though you are not here,
Your memory will live on
For I vow to tell your story,
Till child abuse is gone…

SONG OF SERENITY

Rain
pattering gently
on my roof

is the sound
of rare childhood days
filled with serenity…

WOUNDED

Inside,
a wounded child
still cries
not knowing
that God is listening,
still waiting
to take her hand,
and lead her out
of her inner hell…

AWAKENING

I have no reason to be sad today,
except the sky is dreary, dark, and gray,
but still, the daffodils are in full bloom
and tulips rise in a colorful array.

If I could but define this dismal gloom
that smothers like a musty smoke-filled-room,
I'd open up the door, let in the light,
and sweep the cobwebs out from this old tomb.

The sun will melt away the ghosts of night,
reveal the secrets that I hold so tight,
and offer hope with every brand-new day
so spirit, soul, and body can unite.

LOOKING BACK AT ME

As I look at my reflection, I see much more than it shows.
I see more than just a woman. I see everything she knows.
In her eyes, I see the children who have secrets they must keep,
and I know the fear they feel, and I've cried the tears they weep.
There's a mother who holds tight to every baby that she bore
and she tries so hard to guard them, keep them safe forevermore.
In her heart, she hides the scars from the battles that she's fought
and she re-lives every lesson that this long, hard life has taught.

Look again; I see a woman who, though she's struggled all her life,
sees beauty in each sunrise, and finds challenge in each strife.
She loves with oh, such passion, stands up for what is right,
never surrenders integrity, no matter how hard the fight.
She's a strong yet gentle woman. She's an old soul who'll live on
and for those who chance to meet her, she will never really be gone.
She'll live on inside the hearts and the minds of those who see
what she saw in that reflection that was looking back at me…

HOPE FOR TOMORROW

It seems an eternity ago
a little girl
saw no escape.

Now, on wings
grown out of determination,
she serenely soars

into a new millennium
with renewed hope
that children to come

will not suffer,
will not die,
but transcend

the legacy of abuse...

SONNET-FREE WILL

If I could just go back and change my fate,
turn back the hands of time and know no hate,
rescue a little child from evil's hold,
I'd nurture her before she grew too old.

If life held only cherished memory
and no one had to suffer misery,
how would we understand what's good or bad?
How could we feel what we had never had?

Life is a puzzle filled with mystery
but deep inside we hold a special key
that turns the lock to treasures yet untold
and when it opens, hope and love unfold.

We can't go back but know it's not too late
to use that key to alter our own fate…

CONNECTIONS

Strangers united in life
by fate's tragic hand
offering lessons
to those who understand
common bonds
never planned.

Strangers, unified by pain
revealing indignation
pursuing validation
filled with inspiration

healing day by day
our mutual destination.

FLIGHT PLANS

Someday,
I'll conquer this mountain
and you'll see
just how tough I am

and when I do,
it will be on wings
that carry me beyond
all that was or ever will be,

into a new light...

© SMJ

ABOUT THE AUTHOR

Susan Maree Jeavons is a writer/poet and the former Contributing Editor of Child Abuse and Recovery at Suite101.com where she invited survivors of all types of abuse to talk about their healing journeys.

Susan's work has appeared in numerous online publications, including LadybugBooks.com's Ladybug Flights E-zine, Athena Survivor's Anthology, and Deep Waters where her poem "Gossamer Secrets," won 3rd place out of 302 entries in the 1st poetry contest, and her poem "Immortal Man," won 2nd place in the 2nd poetry contest. LadybugBooks.com also published several of her poems with other poet's work, in a downloadable CD called WOW, Women on A Wire. The proceeds from the sale of the CDs is donated to The National Coalition Against Domestic Violence.

Susan's work has appeared in numerous small presses including the Illinois Prairie Press and the Iowa-Hawkeye Heritage Quilters Guild-Newsletter. *Ball State University published two of Susan 's poems- "Flight Plans" which was first published by LadybugBooks.com, and "Trespasser," in a publication called, "Breaking the Silence," which are used as therapy hand-outs in a sexual abuse group.

The Wisconsin Coalition Against Domestic Violence published her sonnet" Fatal Hand," in their Quarterly Educational Journal. Her poem "Patchwork Memories" was published in the Ideals Publications 2001 Mother's Day Ideals. A Bronx New York high school used her awareness poster, "There Is No Excuse for Child Abuse!" in their National Child Abuse Awareness Month campaign. Philomel Books/Penguin Putnam Inc. published her poem, "Another Rainy Day!" in "I Invited A Dragon To Dinner

And Other Poems To Make You Laugh Out Loud", a children's humorous poetry anthology. In 2003, Susan self-published her first collection of poetry, called Gathering Pearls, A Treasury of Inspirational Poetry.

Since 2014 Susan has been the Administrator of One Day at A Time, Surviving Childhood Abuse, a private website on Facebook for adult survivors of childhood abuse.

* Ball State University is a public research university in Muncie, Indiana. It has two satellite facilities in Fishers and Indianapolis. Susan's poems "Flight Plans" and "Trespasser," which were first published by LadybugBooks.com, were used in their publication called, "Breaking The Silence," which was a therapy hand-out in a sexual abuse group.

BIOGRAPHY

Susan Maree Jeavons is a wife, mother, and grandmother who is passionate about her mission in life. She has transformed a traumatic childhood into an adulthood that is rich in service to her beloved family and to the victims and survivors of child abuse. These poems are about her life and the obstacles she has overcome.

Susan was the Feature Writer for Child Abuse and Recovery at Suite101.com for over 6 years. She wrote monthly articles and commentary on topics related to child abuse. She also published a monthly newsletter and sponsored an annual poetry contest for survivors, and still provides email support for survivors.

Susan's poems have been published at Kota Press: http://www.kotapress.com/, Michael David Coffey's Deep Waters: http://www.geocities.com/Paris/Parc/2331... Ladybug Flights e-zine and in the book Women on A Wire, A Poetry Collection by Ladybug Press http://www.ladybugbooks.com. Susan's poem Another Rainy Day won a nationwide contest and was published by Philomel Books/Penguin Putnam Inc. in the children's humorous poetry anthology I Invited A Dragon to Dinner and Other Poems to Make You Laugh Out Loud. Patchwork Memories was published in the Mother's Day Ideals, A Division of Guideposts, and in The Hawkeye Heritage Quilters Guild Newsletter of Burlington, IA. Her sonnet Fatal Hand was published in the 2000 Quarterly

Journal of the Wisconsin Coalition Against Domestic Violence. Kelly Wallace of Ball State University used Susan's poems Flight Plans and Trespasser in a Sexual Abuse Group as therapy hand-outs.

Susan's book, Gathering Pearls, A Treasury of Inspirational Poetry, is available at Amazon, Borders, Barnes, and Noble, and other bookstores, or by contacting Susan.

Susan was invited to read her poem, *I Am the Child* at the 6th Annual Child Abuse Homicide Victims Candlelight Vigil in Raleigh, NC on Friday, September 28th, 2001. That poem was also used in the Johnson County, North Carolina Child Abuse Prevention Task Force's Blue Ribbon for Kids Campaign. Her poems about child abuse have been used on dozens of websites for survivors.

Other poems are published at The Writer's Voice: http://www.writers-voice.com/, Inscriptions of Hope: http://inscriptionsofhope.com/, and Athena's Survivor's Anthology: http://wuzzle.org/athena/.

Two of Susan's poems were used in the Professional Report: "Reframing Responses-Improving Service Provision to Women Survivors of Childhood Sexual Abuse who Experience Mental Health Problems." © August 2006, by Corinne Henderson-Mental Health Coordinating Council (MHCC) of Sydney, Australia. corinne@mhcc.org.au

Corinne Henderson states that they used Susan's poems; *Musical Lobotomy* and *Trespasser* on page #1 because "they so succinctly reflect the pain and trauma experienced by adult survivors of childhood abuse. We felt it was important to include something in the report that depicted the very personal and yet so widely experienced consequences of abuse."

Susan is also the Founder and Administrator of One Day at a Time, Surviving Childhood Abuse since Sept. 2014. There survivors share their stories in a private and secure place. They are not professionals, just other survivors. Sharing our stories helps to heal all of us.

Your Hope & Faith

Use this page to tell us about your hopes and faith.

YOUR TRUTH

Use this page to excavate your own truth.

MEMORIES, FLASHBACKS, AND PAIN…

Tell us about your memories, flashbacks and pain.

Your Family & Betrayal

Use this page to tell how your family betrayed you.

Your Warrior Spirit

Tell us about your warrior spirit.

Your Appeal to Society

Use this page to appeal to society.

Your Hope & Faith

Use this page to tell us about your hopes and faith.

ACKNOWLEDGMENTS

Flight Plans-Pg. 114- Published in the Ladybug Flights E-Zine and on the CD Women on A Wire, A Poetry Collection by Ladybug Press at http://www.ladybugbooks.com. Proceeds from the sale of the CDs were donated to The National Coalition Against Domestic Violence.

Musical Lobotomy-Pg. 16-published in Kota Press: http://www.kotapress.com/
and at Inscriptions of Hope http://inscriptionsofhope.com/